La Ragazza

Pooja suhag

BookLeaf Publishing
India | USA | UK

Presentation by *BookLeaf Publishing*

Web: www.bookleafpub.com

E-mail: info@bookleafpub.com

ISBN: 9789363311411

First edition 2024

This book is dedicated to my sweet and loving mother and my little niece amber.

ACKNOWLEDGEMENT

I would like to express my deepest gratitude to all those who have supported and inspired me throughout the creation of this poetry book.

To my family, for their unwavering love and encouragement, thank you for being my pillars of strength during both the joyful and challenging times.

To my friends, who have provided endless moments of laughter, solace, and inspiration, your presence has enriched my life in countless ways.

To the readers, who have embarked on this journey through the pages of my poetry, thank you for allowing my words to resonate with you and for finding solace, inspiration, and reflection within these verses.

And finally, to the muse that resides within me, whose whispers of love, sadness, and existential questioning have fueled the creation of these poems, may we continue to explore the depths of human experience together.

With heartfelt appreciation,
Pooja suhag

PREFACE

Welcome to the realm of verse, where emotions swirl, metaphysical ponderings unfold, and the enigmatic quest for the meaning of life finds expression. In this collection of poetry, we embark on a journey through the labyrinth of human experience, exploring the depths of joy, sorrow, love, and everything in between. Human history nowadays is seen as a continuous series of materialistic and engineering marvels. But humans were always more than the environment surrounding them. As the artist inside it could shape the reality in any picture. Here comes the magic of poetry, ranging from Dante's Inferno to Nietzsche's philosophy, that has shaped the course of history and also pushed the boundaries of science a bit further.

Poetry has a unique ability to capture the essence of existence in its most raw and unfiltered form. Poetry doesn't try to solve or attempt to find solutions to the never-ending mysteries of the universe and of course, everyday life but engulf it and make it your part. Not just part, every artistic life lived becomes poetry in itself. Within these pages, you will encounter pieces that delve into the complexities of the human psyche, grappling with questions that have echoed through the corridors of time and in tiny neurons of your brain.

Of course, law, science and mathematics give you a more objective view of the world, a more problem-solving approach. But poetry takes you from the transcendent beauty of nature to the tumultuous depths of the human heart. Each poem invites you to contemplate the mysteries of existence and to find solace in the shared tapestry of our collective consciousness.

As you immerse yourself in these verses, may you discover moments of clarity, inspiration, and profound connection. For in the vast landscape of poetry, there is always a beacon of light to guide us through the darkest of nights and a whisper of truth to accompany us on our journey through life. A journey which often becomes a bit tad boring if lived according to the set rules and followed notions. Little artistic touch in neatly packed together rhymes helps us carry our everyday burden a little better.

TABLE OF CONTENTS

FIRST PART

DREAMS

Oh, hi there,
How all you fare;

Yes, all you are,
who wander somewhere!

Somewhere in bright places;
Sometimes in dark spaces.

All of those who can't sleep;
All the thoughts you are so in deep,

Unfathomable yet so refined;
The secrets that you are out to find,

The search is on;
The night is long,

Alas though, not this time perhaps;
But definitely covered a lot many laps.

Nearer to the shore;
Where this eccentricity makes you lure.

And someday soon,
You will sing this tune;

"Dream fulfilled, oh yes, we said it!
Took a little long;
But at last, we made it!!

THE SELF

You choose your own happiness,
you choose your own pain;
Oh naive creature,
Don't mistake you at the mercy of any game.

The power lies within you,
you are the creator of your weakness,
It's you who chooses, whether to long for light,
Or condemn yourself to bleakness.

When you say yes, it's your own conviction;
And nothing confines you
when you consign yourself to perdition.

You can hold onto things, just as long as you wish,
It is your own calculated neglect, the things that you miss.

It's not far when you will realise, the truths behind;
When you will stop culling fate,
And know that you himself do all those works assigned!

Start thence, to strive to know the meaning, the true call;
Acquaintance with oneself isn't easy after all!

JUST ONE LIFE

Don't cancel that trip every time,
You ain't getting back your prime.
That dress would look pretty on you;
Which you thought 100 times before buying

Don't take that haircut after 3 years,
Don't let yourself be entangled in your nightmares.
Don't let your confidence stoop so low;
Don't let your self-respect take that blow!

Don't wait, start to want,
Go get what you deserve, stop saying "can't!"
What you wished, what you dreamt,
Fulfill this moment, all that you planned.

Stop feeling sorry by accidents,
Stop taking rubbish in.
Take your life hands-on;
Feel smart, having learned things.

Don't settle on mediocrity,
Exert your own free will
It will never be too late
To change what "everyone" thought your fate!!

Don't sit still, don't relay,
Don't give it up, don't delay.
It's a call for action,
A call for today.
A now-or-never game,
In which your "life" is at play!!!

LIFE-MART

Every time there is hope,
Everywhere there is shore
With everyone,
There is love!
And
Everyday there is more!!

With every pain there is gain,
Every struggle makes one sane
Every decision gives way,
To either virtue or to blame.

Every part is a whole,
Every hour is a role,
A prison of sorts;
And happiness, a parole.

Every "emotion" is an art,
In this 'logical' life Mart.
Can't buy "forever bliss"
Can surely "Add to the cart"!

MEANINGS

Meanings we choose to give words
Become what we want them to be!
If you don't believe me,
Follow beneath and you shall see!

Lonely, isolation, solitude, alone;
Let the negative meanings of all begone.
Let's hope to find, let us channelise;
The positive sides, let us analyse.

When you see the rest,
Of what is left;
Weren't you alone,
whenever you slept.

Surely you don't die, whenever you sleep,
Isn't it when loneliness creeps?

Whenever it's with you day or night,
Doesn’t it help you use your utmost might?

Aren't your thoughts only your own;
Isn't it the solitude, where your mind belongs.

Is isolation a phenomenon, or a mere choice?
Grammatically speaking, dear friend
It's not passive but active voice.

Now that we have conquered the triad,
Lonely comes and says with pride;
It's okay if you can win and defend all three,
I can manage on my own;
As they were the branches and I am the tree.

I pondered over and rested my case
with utmost delight,
A tree without branches....
How ALONE my friend,
How poor the plight!

EPHEMERAL LIFE

There is more to people than meets the eye,
Behind those speaking laughter, that silent cry.

Something which probably none can ever know,
As we have mastered the art of putting up a
show.

A show practised continuously, perplex the mind
That we lose the sense of reality, even the urge
to find.

But there comes a point, when that "fake reality"
stifles, shudders and surrenders.
And that's when we got to remember,
There is more to life, love;
Just hold on to it, just don't give up.

The setting sun will rise again,
The darkness will subside;
A new life always awaits you,
In you, walking beside.

SUICIDE

Is that a right?
To let go of all the light
Or a continuous elongated fight
Devoid of any reasons
A fight with inner demons?

Does it become too much,
Or there are no specific reasons as such,
Or do you become too much;
That you so engulf in dark that no light can touch.

Do you feel the breath when,
Decide to give it up for good.
Does it not make any sense then?
Oh, it must have and it should.

That glimmer in those sparkling eyes,
That loudest laughter,
That cry that goes till hell,
That getting better after.

I am sure that must have made quite a sense,
You must have felt what a wonderful lens!

Then what amongst the daily rallying,
Led you to at last failing.
What's your state of mind, little girl,
What didn't let you move, what was that swirl?

Incidents as they are sad and bitter,
No amount of consoling can help those who shatter.
Life while living is good or is it dead better?
These souls have definitely chosen the latter!

And they leave.
And leave behind an eternal question
Are we living for ourselves?
Or always others!
And what is better?
And who is to tell?
And when is the time?
To leave
Or keep living.

LIFE HAPPENS TO US ALL

Every day, every hour, every second.
From being madly in love to just being understanding;

From being mad and furious, to just being disappointed;
From being carefree to being cautious
From being careless to being constraining;

From being naive to being practical,
From being soulful to being a survivor;

From being a fighter to being an adherent.
From being a challenger to being an acceptor;

From being 'you' to being 'someone else',
Life happens to us all!

SEEKING

Happiness, Joy, Elation, Feats;
Eccentric it sounds, but this stops the flow!
It's the pain, suffering, desires and longing,
That keeps you moving, that lets you grow.

No one, absolutely no one, reaches the shore,
without being tested;
And the one who claims to have done so,
Is already, by default, wasted!

Wasted, for they not know the true pleasure;
Having not endured the pain;
All their feats, then make no meaning
All their successes went in vain.

I hope never, to get what I don't achieve
by my hard work and my good deed;
And to any path to salvation, I don't seek,
To wander there, where my belief hasn't me
lead!!

To think of, it's a mystery and a dream then,
The life, which we live at the same time.
Fascinating enough yet cruel others,
It's our inner skirmishes that make it sublime!!

Seek then, the discomfort and uncertainty,
Take sufferings head-on, dive into it plainly;
The "worldly" successes one can't guarantee,
But the "inner "pleasures you will feel certainly!

FRIENDSHIP vs LOVE

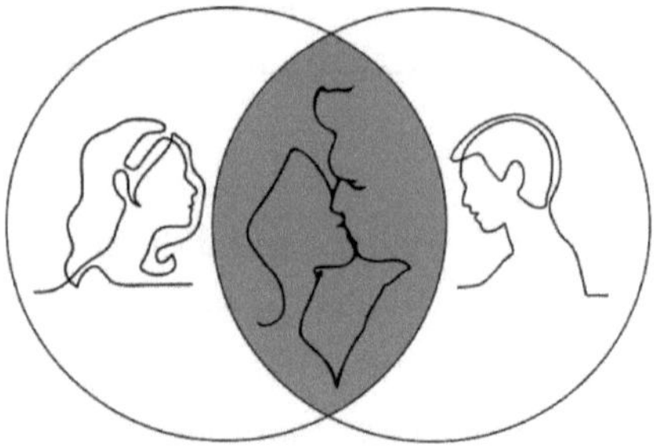

Oh no dear, we can never be friends,
I know there are twitter & instagram trends,
Hashtag friends forever, people as "brands".

For friendship needs time to ripe,
It doesn't 'happn' with a right swipe.

Friendship doesn't crave the attention,
Believes in simple living, not Love's mansion.

Friendship isn't jealous, obsessed,
Doesn't need every time to be caressed.

Friendship grows through vulnerabilities,
Love, poor love, fear such entreaties.

Friendship is rough but nevertheless true,
Love is less the meaning, more the glue.

Friendship is understanding, a room to renew,
Love is the Supreme Court, the last Review.

Friendship doesn't need to be seen just to be felt,
Love is the physical manifestation of all we have dreamt.

Friendship holds onto us,
Love is only there to curse.

Friendship makes us see what we are,
Love makes us become what we never were.

Friendship is "I am there, but be careful"
Love is, "you have made my life miserable."

Friendship is YOU, just the better,
Love is, my dear, always the other!!

LOST IN LABELS!!

What's the point of rising from the dust
When you can no longer appreciate your firsts
When you have achieved high labels and laurels
But you have failed at life's real tests

The hand-to-mouth situation
That must have fed your creation
That poverty-stricken strife
If don't come first at appreciation

You have failed at your attitude
If it doesn't come with gratitude
You have got it all wrong
If you let go of the headwinds that made you strong

Flaunting the number of zeroes in your bank accounts
Follower of lessons that capitalism propounds
You magnanimously failed at real earnings
Howsoever illogical it sounds

If you utter mean and wear pride
If you lost your soul in this nonsensical ride
If you run behind this crazy facade
If you are driven by the utterly blinded charade

When old friends become subjects to laugh
When the dressed-up, good English becomes
your only class
When you feel you have achieved everything
and all
Precisely then, my dear, you are destined to fall,
When you begin to think you are no longer
"small"!

LIFE IS STRANGE

Beautiful, sometimes, and scary others
Encrypted in ambiguity, all it covers

Utter bold sometimes, craziness at its peak
Others, just pain in the joints and heart just weak

Full of surprises sometimes
seem like a battle you are out to win
Others just simple shocks
when you feel like drowning it in gin.

The meaning you search, it's all in vain
Extreme pleasure sometimes, other ecstatic pain

Sometimes it's the journey
Others, a quest to reach the end
Sometimes it's always the origin
Others it's just what's in the trend.

MIRROR

The myths and the unpopularity,
The moment we get that clarity,

When we attain the unattainable;
When we walk together in solidarity.

When we see it within, when we say it without,
That exact moment when we hear it aloud,

When the whole is one and the one is whole;
We realize what this self is all about.

We read so much, to always know it more,
We fight so much to reach to the core,

How to fail illusion, how to be enlighten;
We forget looking at the stars while longing for the shore.

God, beauty, peace and depth,
It’s all-encompassing, it's all in your breath,

You know it when you see that light;
Nothing shines brighter than what's inside.

THE ENIGMA!

It's a delight to see the life around,
The motion, the happiness, the pride;
And sad how the same life too confound,
The fear, the poverty, the strife.

Much less it demands, even less is given, How
strange life is, "expectations driven".

It doesn't get along with anyone,
not at least for long,
It waits for death only,
where it truly belongs.

No matter what you do,
Can never impress it,
Pain, suffering are all its part
Can never suppress it.

If it's history it will repeat,
if it's economy its bold,
If it's environment it's natural,
if it's polity it's old.

The only and good thing about it then,
Oh, listen, all men and women;
That it's beautiful nonetheless,
Eccentric in it's ways, least a plan!

FLAWED NOTIONS

How profound these pleasantries & positivities are
That we keep on chasing near and far
Are they even pleasant? Are they even positive?
For which we indulge in a continuous war

Is the good really good?
Is the bad actually bad?
Is it always the failures?
That really makes us sad.

Why do we always choose?
Comfort of the known
Isn't the leap of faith in the unknown
That really makes us groom

The happiness that we keep on pursuing
Do we really know its nature?
isn't it the suffering and pain alone
That makes us a wiser creature.

The riches that we boast of
Is it really the important side?
Those relationships that stand by us
Doesn’t that count as the real pride?

Success that breeds satisfaction
Satisfaction that breeds stagnation
In our book of what’s right and wrong
Don’t we all need an alteration.

TIME AND CHANGE

The sunset will remain the same and so will the sunrise,
The laughter will remain the same and so will the cries,
Same will remain opinions of people for us and ours of them;
The truths will remain the same and same will remain those lies!

The peace will remain the same, and so will remain the unrest,
The failing would remain the same and so will remain the success,
Same will remain the tragedy—comedy phases in and out;
The dawn will remain the same, and same will remain the dusk!

The questions will remain the same, and same will remain the doubts,
The clear skies will remain the same and so will remain the clouds,
Same will remain your fantasies, your wishes and dreams,
The love will remain the same and same will remain the loads!

Nothing really changes, no one really changes, thus
Changes only then, is the notion of change for us.

INCOMPREHENSIBLE FEELINGS

Man dreads the future being so uncertain
He chooses it too wisely but all in vain
In situations like these, he most certainly then is
doomed to be fooled and destined to fail!

For matters of the heart aren't for the mind to
dictate
All his efforts therefore evidently go to waste

It must flow and flow endlessly.
Like that of a river.
And it must be fragrant in all its essence;
Like that of a blossoming flower.

And it can't limit, for it's infinite;
And it can't cease, for it's power and might

It can't be circumscribed in mere words.
It's all-encompassing feelings,
Not just pleasure but equally the hurt
Happy is the body to which it binds
The sensations outgrow the cognitive abilities of the mind.

And in that moment, you realise,
There is nothing more powerful and serene and wise

It is the seeking that sets everything right;
It is that ecstatic feeling, and it is that light!

It is everything below and everything above
Incomprehensible feelings which we fondly call "LOVE"

MAKE LIFE A DANCE

Live it to the fullest,
Enjoy even the still;
Connect to the mind,
And power your "will"

Seek through, concentrate high,
Make beautiful the path you ply.
Do observe, Do attach,
To this moment, to this pledge.

All laughter ain’t happiness,
All tears aren’t sad!
The journey itself is bliss,
That you must cautiously tread.

Don't you just look outside,
Look inside yourself, too;

Times, you engulf the nature,
Other, let nature behold you.

Sleep tight, work light,
Challenge storm, channelise "quiet".
Laugh aloud and smile every time,
Let peace betray you and then you must shine.

Walk into the trees, walk into the deep,
Say bye to the past and make it all sweep.

Be in the being, be here and now,
Immerse into you and take this vow;

Make easy, the "difficult",
Make pain, the chance
Make life, oh sweetheart!!
Make life a dance.

Aim for the sky,
Standing on the ground,
Make living and happy,
Everything you surround.

Make happy the countenance,
Make happier the trend;
Make happy the beginning,
Make happier the end.

Existential Dread

Every now and then, I ask this question to me
Are we really living a life? And if it's free!
Now-a-days existential crisis everyday
No more," oh results are due, I have got to
pray?"

Question of " What is life" is pressing me to the
core
"Did my baby have dinner?" Who is even asking
anymore?

Got to live every second. Work hard. Party
harder.
The notions as such are day by day getting
blurred

Does god even exist? If yes, how do you reach him? Is there some kind of ladder?

Anxiety, depression, oh how hard I laughed
In my prime, how miserably I failed to grasp
The littleness of life
And abstractness of its meaning
I was doomed to an eternal state of despair
The day when “this” I realized!

THE GIRL CHILD!

Desires to see the world,
When they first unfurled;
Fancied all the beauties,
In the womb as I swirled!

In that safe haven, 9 months I waited,
Patiently, gently and utmost elated
Dizziness though honestly scared me sometimes;
Trusted my bearer, she would endure those
times.

Finally the wait was almost over,
And I was going to be blessed with a love
shower.
Was longing to see the outside world,
Feel the affections, I for so long yearned.

That was when that lesson I learnt,
My nascent dreams tragically were burnt;
Pitied! A girl... that too first,
"And I was born and I was cursed."

I was in shock, I asked so many "whys"
I gave my all, I did all possible tries.
To know what was wrong with me;
And to change it and make me free.

I wanted not heaven, just a little less hell.
I wanted not freedom, just not a commodity to sell.
I wanted not equality, just to be respected.
I wanted not to challenge, just to be accepted.

But I grew up never really knowing.
I grew up, like an endless river flowing
The answer was straight and the gesture sublime
why you have issues with trust?
"Well, when I was born, I was cursed!"

THE CHOICE!

The history behind us,
The economy foresees us;
How much we travelled, how far do we go?
This "development" blinds us.

The polity that scares us,
The geography that amazes us;
The environment that we betray,
The science that betrays us!

The mathematics that puzzles us,
The statistics that deceive us;
The theory that helps us,
The emotions that precede us.

The choices we have,
The choices we had;

But what changed, then what changed,
Just getting worse from bad.

The living and the dead,
The begotten, the beget;
The constant and the continuous,
The easy and the arduous.

Is that the end, is that all,
Do we give up, do we hold on;
For we humans are a crazy race,
Just tell us, for "How" long!

VOIDS

Challenges, choices;
Confusions, constraints.
Deep demanding desperate drains
Within without everywhere everytime;
Blemishes brainwashing belittling blames.

Severity stigma suffocation sways,
Pride paranoia perpetual pain.
Lies lives languishing layers,
Audacity bluffs pretentious prayers!

Fear fanatics fragmented frays,
Customising choosing casting clays;
Rigorous rattling randomised race,
Testing tumbling treacherous days.

Dreaming, dying, creating, destroying,
Shores peaks plains ravine,
Future is shallow and nature is fragile;
As voids augment, as voids align!

SECOND PART

NICETIES OF ROMANCE

"Hi," the text was sent!
A little reservedly and after some mind makeup,
"Hello," the answer went.

Within seconds the conversation led way,
Exciting, somewhat shy,
But a highly determinative sway.
"I like this, you like what?"
All other errands put to stay!

Laughter and expressions,
Adorations, mentions;
The days went by,
And the night turned into day.

One month went,
And then four,
And now they are close;
Like never before!

Shared much,
And fought a little;
Life seemed perfect,
No grievances as such.

As the time passed on,
The definition that 'term' held,
Changed its zone.
From being available at all times;
It got comfortable in the backseat rhymes,

Trusting the managing wheels,
Set by time
And polished by those innocent feels!!

Not long before the order disarrayed,
When the connection became more of a trade,
Love still at heart, but heart was broken;
Ego splashed right through the words spoken!

"Enough," said one.
Reply came, "I too am 'done'!"
Parted ways;
And there ended a story,
That once was the most beautiful phase!

CHANCE-CHANGE

Met them by chance,
Infatuation at that very first glance!
Before I knew, I was caught in that fray,
Those lips were muttering something, I reckon
But those glaring eyes constantly held sway!

Few months into it,
I started feeling this part in-depth a bit!
One day, they say you changed,
And now you don't fit!

But what's the point of not changing, I said
I didn't know you initially,
That's why that eagerness and intrigue,
That's why those "looking forward" to meet,

That's why those never-ending calls,
And that's why those stroll in malls!

No rocket science, just around “6 month getting along” drive!
To get to know each other well,
At least enough to know whether it will thrive.

And then it comes naturally, to a normalized pace;
Because life is to enjoy slowly, it’s not any race!

The talks become limited,
The enthusiasm settles.
Relationship takes another shape and form,
Now other priorities also pedals!

Then why this anxiety and why this fear,
When both of them know it’s a necessity mere!
It’s not the “non-attention” it’s just the standard shifting,
Then why does one’s ego always need lifting!

It’s perhaps the most difficult phase to rationalize,
Only if handled maturely, then lay the prize!
The prize of eternal love and affection,
Which stems from long lasting perfect imperfection!!

But the sad part is getting stuck in this loop,
When that established admiration starts
demanding proof;
Leading to intrusions and constant ego strife,
The attraction dies and the distrust comes alive!

It's exactly when the two make a decision,
Tries to reason this with their utmost precision!
Then it's that pure simple intention that leads the
way forwards!
Either it's the end or a new start again that day
onwards!

I LOVE YOU

'I LOVE YOU.'
says, She to Him.
'Oh', he replied,
And in shock, he sat,
but how did it come to that?
Didn’t we have a pact?

Remember, to be "friends"
then, oh poor girl,
why such errands.

He looked attentively at her,
hoping she would too concur.

But she let it all out that day,
didn't know what else was there to say.

He went ahead,
to address her visions,
to clarifications and to reasons.

He said aloud, wasn't it always clear,
then why on earth, that I should bear.

she stands there 'still', not even a word,
wanting to get freed, poor caged bird.

Sensing this, he again tried,
Failed soon, when she at last cried.

And said to him,
with utmost humility;
Yes, it was clear and I admire your civility.

But now I don't see if I can keep,
The promises made to you,
please let me go then,
And finally bid adieu.

HAVE YOU FOUND THEM

"Have you found them?"

When you will, you won't just smile,
You will laugh your heart out,
And it won't be just momentarily,
That happiness is what your soul will shout!

You will cry the tears of joy,
And not because of them;
It's for them that you will ever cry.

"Have you found them?"

When you will, the ups and downs will remain,
The sufferings will be there and so will be the pain;
But you would not once feel weak, rather stronger!
And you will fight with zeal howsoever longer.

"Have you found them?"

When you find them, you will feel alive every moment,
There may be little scuffles, never the never-ending torment.
You'll crave for them with all of you,
And whatever you had dreamt;
Everything will, one by one, come out to be true.

"Have you found them?"

With them, you would not feel the need to be 'fancy'
Outwardly;
You can be your own self and that too loudly!

You will feel one with their presence,
With them you will be at ease;
The eyes will shine with all that's there,
And the whole world would freeze!

"Have you found them?"

And if you still have not,
Worry not!
As no age is set,
You wait for them;
Cause life is not short!

It will all make sense,
What it's all about;
And when you will find the one,
You will not have any single doubt!

HOW LONG?

How much we can linger on the case,
How far can we wander from the base?
When death has a standing warrant against each
How long can we stop that threshold to breach?

How long the institutionalised facades will go,
The capitalism, communism, the political show!
How far we can let this deception prolong;
How long till to the ultimate reality we will
bow?

Amidst those makeshifts beliefs and societal
convictions,
Making us feel worthy, all those paid
subscriptions

How many generations will still be in denial?
How long till we see it was we who were on trial!

And yes, it's always been the same as it seemed before.
These trivialities, oh right, they always have us allure.
How long till we find the real purpose behind;
How long will be the time, when in us, the “us” we’ll find!

ANOTHER YEAR

And when the dust settles
It's all the same day-to-day battles
When the outward is put together
And the inside continuously rattles

Times when we seek back our cradles
To beat those storms, we everyday pedals
Sometimes we are broke,
Others are laurels, medals!!

And living among all those realities
We make sense of all those cruelties
Oscillations of fear and being fine
We step into another life one day at a time

Give ourselves another chance
On tunes of life, we learn to dance
To stand up once again
To have our end of the bargain

And yet again we plan far and near
With a bright smile and heavy hope
We wish each other a happy new year!

YOU and YOU!

And one fine day
In that summery May
A person with a familiar countenance
Stopped me at midway entrance
She smiled at me
As if long-known
Her eyes saw me with a shimmer
As if her child has grown
I smiled back at her
And tried to understand
The face I was looking
The words that were flickering
The hands that were shaking
The eyes that were glimmering
she recognised me instantly
Talked to me with an air of familiarity

Asked me about how was I doing
If I manage my emotions well
Or am I still the same annoying?
Further she went
When even more she vent
How did I manage the new life traumas
How I deal with everyday's dilemma
I was surprised at first and annoyed later
Who is she? Why to her whims, I cater!
She was indeed behaving intrusive
But those questions were quite pensive
I tried to walk away but she followed
introduced herself as the "time I borrowed"
I was perplexed, amazed and shocked
How dare she with such authority, talked .
I stopped and faced
And in a tough tone, a question I raised
"Time borrowed? "What does that mean
Mistaking me for someone else.
Someone else have you seen
And I walked by, turning my head,
"I am the path you once used to tread
I am the pieces of you, all shreds
I am the familiar unfamiliarity
I am the ghostly real reality
I was weak and suffering
But I was proud and uttering
Self-love and a little naive
For the relationships I would anyway dive"

I was getting the hints
My mind was sharing the print
Alongside as she said
"Did I meet her, HER, whom I dread?"
I thought I moved on
Is she some con? l again saw her eyes
There were no absolute lies
And I understood it at last
She was ME, she was MY past!
She held her head with wisely pride
She knew I recognised her
There is nothing more to hide
I was scared to acknowledge
But she was way more mature
The stubbornness was gone
The politeness replaced the furore
Gently she smiled
And on reason she relied
To address and show me
There is nothing to fear anymore
As only in face you are my clone
And before she left, she said,
"I am glad you now know how to move on."

SUBLIME LOVE

Love, it isn't about Roses and Valentine,
Trust me,
"Companionship" works just fine!

But easier said than done,
Because this word holds emotions more than
one!

It never is loud, maybe sometimes shy,
It calms your nerves, every time you cry!

Consistent and persistent in efforts,
No situational strides,
And when you feel almost on the edge;
Pushes you, to just give one more try.

It likes you in every mood,
Embraces your past, today, tomorrow;

Dances along in happiness;
Saddens with your sorrow!

You don't need to look for it,
It comes naturally as you grow,
And when this sublimity strikes;
I guarantee you will know!

SOMEONE

Be a person bigger than your mind,
Even if there is no reason to find.

Be someone who forgives,
Be someone who forgets;
Be someone who likes from heart,
Be someone who enjoys life-fest!

Be someone who is kind,
Someone who regrets being rude.
Who initiates healthy conversations,
Someone not shrewd!

Life is testing for us all,
Everyone suffers from some kind of pains,
Be someone not judgemental;
Be someone free from pretentious gains!

Be someone who thinks but not judge,
Who stays even if it hurts!
Because in the end,
Life takes a bend.

The pain goes away,
And the anger fades.
Life shines more,
And offer brighter shades!

And then we realise,
What remains on another side too;
Is a person,
Just as you!

So,
Before it's too late,
In this limited time frame;
Be someone who is a true mate!

Be kind and love selflessly,
Don't let loose random emotional sway;
Believe in yourself. In natural instincts.
Cause in the end,
Love always finds its way!

MOTHER

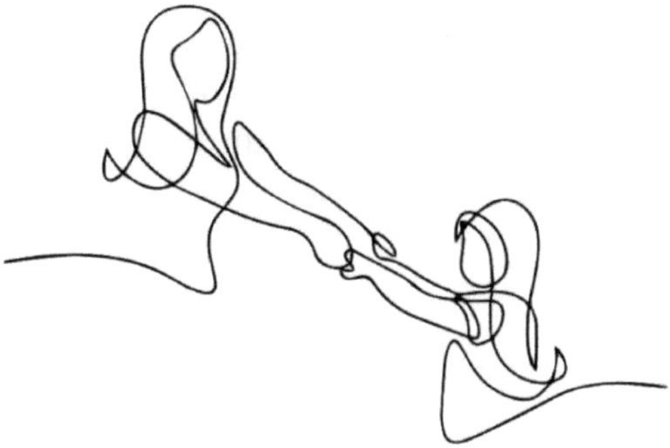

The Divine creature,
The loveliest soul;
The Super Mom,
With a plenteous role!

The dignity she embraces,
The sweetness she beholds;
Oh mother, what can I say,
She is the glitter, she is the gold.

The longings she admired,
The dreams she chose;
To fulfil our desires,
She gave up all those!

The ever-laughing, the never-complaining,
She lives through all days;

The smile on her beautiful face,
Trumps even the sun's rays.

Always beaming dusk to dawn,
No fear, self-doubt, not an inch of pride,
If there exists any heaven at all;
She is that earthly paradise.

A HOME

Big doors and open windows
Greenery of all sorts
That is practically, what I conceived
When I thought of a dream home

A home where all my fancies lie
A home where all my atoms smile
A home where my soul resides
A home where even my efforts try

A home where my love is free
A home where my shyness glee
A home where my nature nurtures
A home where my capacity ventures

A home through beginnings and ends
When I feel weak, still tall it stands
A home when life hits me
In the warmth of it, is where I land.

JUST SOMETIMES!

Otherwise I am happy always,
Years, months or days,
It is just sometimes;
That I actually "break".

Otherwise I keep my calm,
And I remain composed,
It is just sometimes;
That real "me" is exposed.

Otherwise I accept the challenges,
And I am always strong,
It is just sometimes;
That things go wrong.

Otherwise I laugh a lot,
Like I am always in my prime,
It is just sometimes;
That I commit a crime.

Otherwise I am very cheerful,
And all down to earth,
It is just sometimes;
That I question my worth.

Otherwise I am all you can love,
And I am all you can want,
It is just sometimes;
That you regret that grant!

A LOVE STORY

For the heart so flailing,
For the eyes so glaring,
For the reasons so appealing,
She starts him emailing,
"Hello there, how are you feeling?"

Not much time elapsed,
When her phone again flashed,
Seeing notification, she flapped,
Eyes shocked and beats enhanced,
To open or not, her mind entrapped.

At last she rang conviction bell,
To let it heaven or be it hell,
She wanted to see what he got to tell,
So she made up her mind and opened the cell
"Hello there, I am doing well."

And there then started a beautiful tale
Towards the shore, the ship started to sail
Two became one, their connection nonpareil
Holding hands tightly they walked towards the aisle
It's not the stories but the love that we hail!

LOVE WEEK

Good or bad?
Excited or trend!

Romance or commerce;
Pure or pretensions!

Loving and feeling.
Or just handy dealing.

Craziness and Obsessions.
Or just fancy creations?

Celebrating the gist;
Or surviving a pulsating wrist!

Because they are special?
Or it's just a vessel!

Because vows are rusting!
Because everybody is posting!!

Long-lasting? Or Just a week's affair?
Well, Instagram says ….
Love is in the air!

I WONDER

I wonder, how would it feel?
To not be able to live up to one's zeal
To not be able to open one's heart
To never really knowing where to start

To always struggle, to falter, and surrender
I wonder, how would it feel?
To see one's own life put asunder

To giving up amidst never-ending atrocity
How would it feel to surrender one curiosity?

To not being answered, despite forever pray
To slowly but clearly see one's life passing away

I wonder, how would it feel
To always restart and restart?
When you're not its artist
But your life is an art!

THIS OR THAT

Take the chance, throw yourself into the
unknown
Either you sail through or you drown.

You either conquer or you lose,
If you don't win,
you have to choose.

Either to accept that failure, surrender,
or to suffer painfully under resistance.

But choose what you may,
This my dear is a simple play.

When you win, you feel that immense pleasure,
when you lose, you feel that immense pain.
For, emotions behind ecstasy and suffering
Are indeed the same!

Both make you feel alive,
Both give life meaning.
It's the utmost faith in oneself
It's the innermost believing

Choose thence, either 'this' or 'that',
Never the in-between leaning!

ADDRESSES

Addresses reflecting a shy ill prepared girl
Taking small steps in this unending swirl

Addresses with a sense of belongingness with friends
Addresses that showed her famous and latest trends

Addresses that found first and last love
Addresses that took the eternity vows

Addresses that trembled and made her weak
Addresses that let her curiosities tweak

Addresses that forced her to choose and swore
Addresses that made her stronger than before

Addresses that became home away from home
Addresses that were peace and natures dome

Addresses that made her futuristic and learn from her past
Addresses that made her a way, a way that would last.

CONFIDANTE

When I am happy,
She is happier than me;
When I am sad,
She is miserable than me!

When I feel alone,
She cares for me;
When I feel content,
She cheers for me!

When I am excited,
She reciprocates;
When I am depressed,
She ameliorates!

She has been my constant past,
Without her I don't want my future to last!

She is pretty and kind,
caring and quiet;
Makes my days worth living,
Her mere sight!!

Presence benign, soul divine,
In all situations, she always shines!
May she get everything she desires,
Even if she is crying, cries with glee!
And May god always bless her;
Just as the way she blesses me.

A COMPLEXITY

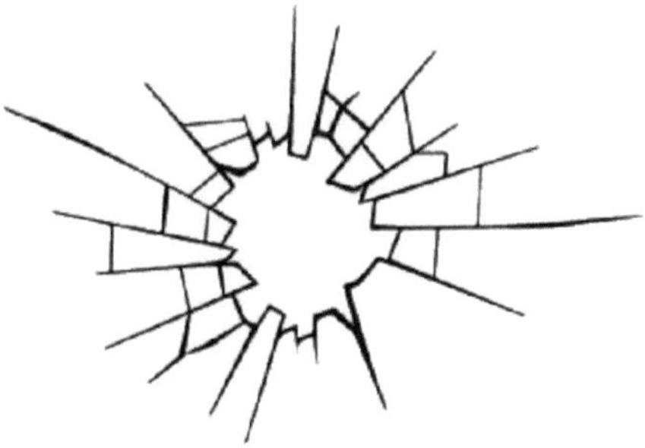

What is that which you seek,
Is it lucid or is it bleak;
Know if it's real or just a wish
Is it strong or is it weak?

Difficult to understand, impossible to read,
Amongst few flowers, so many weed
How much you try to comprehend,
Binds you so tight, crave to get freed.

Comes often in your way, no matter the place,
The privilege, the problems, or the populace,
Captures your mind, deepens your thoughts;
You try your level best to find solace.

Does it have any cure, or is it just a phase,
I just sometimes ponder, how long, how many
days

Keep the secrets, bide the time,
Just wish someday, coming out of the maze!

A GIRL

Once upon a time,
There was a girl, in her prime,

Of medium height but high aspirations,
Of shy attitude but least speculations.

Of big eyes but small face,
Of reality checks alongside imaginations.
She walked swiftly, she smiled gracefully,
Of reserved nature, but no hesitations.

She was confident, and smart and brave,
Yet was vulnerable, despite calculations.
She listened to others, with all powers,
And talked to herself, for long long hours.

At times, she too felt alone,
For sympathies, she too was prone.
But one thing she definitely knew to be true,
That no matter what, life goes on.

FOR ONCE

Let's be grateful for once,
For what we have
Not what we could have bought;
For once, let's just pray,
Just thank the "is" not think the "ought".

Let's revere for once and cherish and hope,
For these aren't mere words,
Sisyphus would say it;
It is the "mountain" and it is the "slope".

It's about time and it never is,
For once let's just see and not blink;

Don't seek mountain, don't seek river,
It's within you that you fall and you sink.

For once let's respect the harmony,
For once, not glorify the chaos.
Let's stop the rhetoric, the "stylized words"
Let’s know who we are, not caged birds.

For once let's take responsibility.
For once let's have empathy,
For once let's just stop debating on what seems right but do the right.
Let's just be "Humans", for once!

THIRD PART

RANDOM ACCESS MEMORIES

Accidentally I reckon,
The beach we met on.
Your second and mine first,
Blink of an eye, an instant trust.
I considered me a fictional character;
Oh, has it come true!!!
I could hear the rhythms going awry..
Did you hear the guitars too?

That sepia sunset, that starry sky;
That eye contact at the café, that beautiful "HI".
That walk in the sand, the random salsa dance,
The Ghalib ki poetry, that Dostoevsky's France.
The philosophy of Nietzsche;
The total absence of cliches!

The running ahead of time,
The feeling of utmost prime.
The aligned interests,
The bojack horseman show,
Not even a day and it already started to grow.

Am I in a dream?
Is this a bigger scheme!
Am I thinking too much;
This never happened as such.

It was effortlessly plain,
The emotions that swayed.
Awestruck was that moment;
That bliss knew no bounds..
Yes it was as strange,
As strange as it sounds!

HEY YOU

I feel special when you are around;
Like I found eternity, like I'm abound.

The comfort, the feeling, the sense of feeling free;
Your presence, it's indeed, that makes me "ME".

Years spent and ages to go;
Oh I remember, I still tease you as "bro"!

With you only,
I yearn to see the lights, the mountains and the breeze;
With you only,
I want the time to both flow and cease.

Deep down I know,
Deep down this show;
That life isn't pleasurable,
It is just with YOU, that I glow.

The sense to feel alive,
The feel to see you smile,
Perhaps I'm in Heaven;
And Heaven is here to thrive!

Words fail to describe you, I still tried;
Be my groom and I shall be your bride.

THE 3,13 AND 23

When I was 3 years old, I hardly remember how I was,
Although Soft skin and big eyes, the photos do have their course,
But the dilemmas working inside that little heart;
Reckoning those, I'm still at a loss!
But rounding off that passive phase,
I was maybe a little introverted child in those days.

10 years later, I celebrated my birthday turning thirteen,
That standard protocol of school, giving toffees, chocolates, that day I was definitely a "celebrity teen"!

But the memories now were sharpened perhaps,
As I felt all those struggles & real time traps!

when I turned 23, college was at the peak,
There was so much I had already learned
So much was out there that I was eager to seek
It was a time, of more relax and less stress;
Cause you are so positive, even if you failed,
you have that energy to always start afresh!

And I am 29 now, sometimes stuck, sometimes free,
I feel I am all at once, the 3,13 and twenty three!!
There is eagerness and then there is charm,
Then there is prolonged chaos but refreshing balm!
But all in all, I found it a never-ending journey,
Sometimes, it rains heavily and sometimes it's sunny

Living on the edge some days and then a prolonged slumber,
But true to as they say it, "age is just a number"!!

PERHAPS SOMEDAY!!

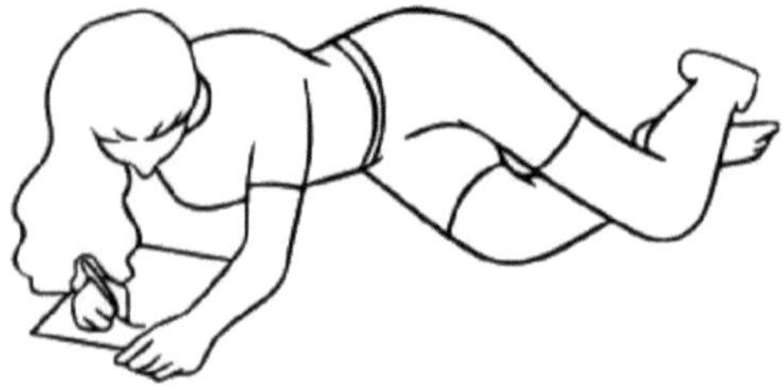

I think perhaps someday….
I might tell you,
What I felt then,
What I wished…
And what I dreamt!
About us.
About planning the future together;
About getting over each other's past together.
About life!
And about love.
Sharing our professional feats;
And our kids mark sheets.
Holding hands.
Taking strolls in the front park;
About going to friends weddings,
And gossiping about breakups, endings..!
About how much I admire you, everyday, About those little sweet memories I cherish! Admit my love to you day and night.

And saying it aloud you make my life bright.
Someday……
But you are lost to me.
Not just the physical presence,
Even your benign essence!
I don't recognise you no more,
You are a stranger with furore.
You are not that someone I met;
You are a riddle I don't get.
You are that classic lesson people call;
For which I ignorantly took fall.
May be not so ignorant, as much belief!
Belief in love and belief in hope;
Hanging on to that bruised rope.
But it feels relief,
Letting go.
To take it slow, this time
To not push
To just let it flow!!

WHAT AM I?

Sometimes I wish to write something that's never been written before;
Sometimes I wish to think that has never before pondered upon;

Sometimes I wish to see life from an entirely new perspective;
Sometimes I wish to feel sadness too as attractive.

Sometimes I long for a day that never really ends;
Sometimes I wish to be myself and not societal trends.

Sometimes I wish my heart to calculate and my mind feels.

Sometimes I wish my body gets numb and my
soul chills.

Sometimes I wish I move on in an instant;
Sometimes I wish there is some constant.

I want to be this, and I want to be that.
Today I'm me, tomorrow someone else.

This is precisely what I am,
This is precisely what you are.
Formidable enough to never be known;
Easiest gamble to put your money on.

SOMETIMES, OTHERS!

Sometimes I miss you;
Others, just good books!
Sometimes, I admire the soul;
Others, just pure looks!

Sometimes I need you,
Others, just me, even more!
Sometimes, I think plain;
Others, the abstract lure!

Sometimes, I think I love,
Others, I know I live.
Sometimes, I think I deserve,
Others, I'm all there to give!

Sometimes, I ponder over stuff,
Others, I sit still!
Sometimes, I regret my decisions,
Others, I see through every bluff!

Sometimes, I like being free,
Others, I crave cage!
Sometimes, I am most ardent,
Others, it's wild rage!

Sometimes, I like being me,
Others, the search is endless!
And although I try a lot,
But still somehow, I end up careless!

And between these sometimes and others;
There is life and death.
Several not just one;
As many demise as there are breath!

I WISH

I wish there existed words for all that I felt;
I wish there was a forum where all my dilemmas were dealt.

I wish I could just see and separate the truth from the lies;
I wish someone could touch the soul by just looking into the eyes!

I wish I was born and then reborn every second,
I wish I could live everyday and then store it in the backend.

I wish I could do better than I did the previous day,
I wish I could speak all that my heart has to say.

I wish Boundaries some days and others
abundantly free;
I wish Sometimes I want you and others you
crave me!

I wish ‘this’ today and I wish ‘that’ tomorrow;
Sometimes ecstasy, sometimes deep sorrow.

Living and loving,
Striving and feeling,
Each moment a completeness;
That’s what gives life meaning!!

WISHED FOR.... DREAMT OF!

You are everything that I wished for,
You are everything that I dreamt of!

You are that shining bright sunny day,
You are the beautiful rain in a cloudy May!

You are that benign blooming flower,
You are that fresh morning shower!

You are those dew drops on the haze,
You are my "all smiles day and night" phase!

You are the painting that cuts into deep,
You are the poetry that makes one weep!

You are loving and gentle and kind, and caring,
You are successful and keen, involved and daring !

With you, it's easy, just how a river flows,
Like how a newborn cries, like how a seed grows!

I cherish with you every dusk and dawn,
Today, tomorrow wherever I go!

I hope it's there even if we aren't anymore,
I feel love with you in all its forms!

And yes.
You are everything that I wished for,
You are everything that I dreamt of!

AND WHAT IF

What if I had not let myself be subdued?
Raised my voice and behaved more crude?
What if I had not strangulated my dreams?
What if I had not silenced those screams?

What if I had let my imagination fly?
Had my opinions, my flirtations try?
What if I had danced with my inner child?
What if I had made my essence, feel more wild?

What if I had cried out loud when I was caged?
Let my inner voice shout and not well-behaved
What if I had preserved my memories albeit sad?
What if I had pursued my heart while ditching the plans!

What if I had sat once, sat still?
Out of that chaos, out of that drill.
What if I had thought and not been tricked?
What if I had said on my deathbed
That I have lived?

AWAKE IN DREAM

Yesterday night, she had a brief sleep
Short, yet crisp, but a clear long dream

A fairy tale of sorts
Beautiful but coarse

A princess dressed in white
Habituated to do everything right
Proud, but dependent
Waiting for someone with power and might

Innocence at its best
Ready to pass all tests
To stand up to his eyes
To worship him without rest

One day, she did find one
For whom all the arts she did learn
Got ready to surrender all those
And let his love alone made her burn

Dreaming of love castles, she tagged along
Leaving behind even her own self where she
used to belong,

Flowers in hand and expectations at heart
A grand city life, where stopped her cart

Stepped onto not just a new person
She stepped into a different world
The unfamiliar sky made her grim
The commotions made her swirl

Confused and scared, she held his hand tighter
If the outside is scary, the inside would make her
feel lighter

Entered a large dome
Empty with filled furniture
Servants at her service all the time
But none to care and everything else just blur

The outside, with which she was scared
The inside with which she was betrayed
To let go of these shackles
That's what for every day, she prayed

But praying did not really help
And she was there all alone and stuck
And just then she was about to lose hope
A loud bang, she heard at her doorstep

She woke up, and the dream had vanished
A chill was still there but the senses now she cherished

She gathered herself up and made herself tea
As strong as it could be, to not let her again sleep
She was glad she was awake, breathed a sigh of relief
Never knowing she is just awake to the “dreams” of her beliefs!!!

ABYSS!

Sometimes on those sleepless nights
I think
When my eyes are closed
but my eyes don't blink

When I could hear the sound of my breath
And my heart starts to shrink
Starts to sink deeper amidst
Stars all around and then there is an abyss

An endless hollow space twinkling
I hear my voice even when I wasn't speaking
And I dare to look around
In this space in which I was abound

Everywhere there is nothingness
A step towards embracing akinness

I try to reach a shore or at least an end
Or if not then a route to which I bend

But I was going on and on
And I walked for hours and the time begone
I looked back, I looked straight
Paused and thought, "it isn't looking great"

What is it? Another question
To me, from me
My heart was beating calmly
My body feeling genuine glee

There were so many questions
And a path that was struck
For a girl like me
Who would have every opportunity pluck

This wasn't good but it felt like one
Felt like ecstasy felt like love

And I sat there, still
My body, I couldn't feel anymore
Something was beating around indeed for sure
But I couldn't less care!

And I could not see anything just the air
Air amidst all other AIRS!
And when I finally opened my eyes

I was a different person altogether
As if my life had opened its layers......

SO ALIVE

Falling rain and opened doors,
Distracted me from daily chores;
The smell filled my heart,
The beauty filled my eyes,
So, I kept everything aside;
And I looked and I smiled.

I felt my breath, my body and my soul,
And I felt so alive
And I felt so alive!!

Opening the doors
The sense in me arose
Of eternal and infinite
The rain singing a prose

I danced to the tune
The life in me grew
With every passing second
The essence seemed true.

I felt my soul, my veins and pride
And I felt so alive
And I felt so alive.

A LONGING OR A FACADE

And what was I thinking?
When I still held on to you while I was sinking!
When I trusted you without a blink;
When I was giving you all at the cost of
shrinking.

You came and became my everything,
With you I felt like sharing,
You promised to break my "broken heart legacy"
That I was, for so long, carrying!!

Your assurances seemed honest,
Your intentions pure and truest!
Believe it or not, with you,
I opened my heart to the fullest!

Then what was it that laid before my eyes?
Was it that my trust taken for a ride?
Was it simply a blot of deception,
Or was it all along a planned oblivious
perception!

And now, I think about it all,
How this large a world is in fact so small.
How much I have already experienced,
How much is still left to be discerned!

But the question remains unanswered,
When will this end, this quest? This yearn!
Am I wisely earning from my experiences?
Or my experiences say I have so much yet to
learn!

RESTART

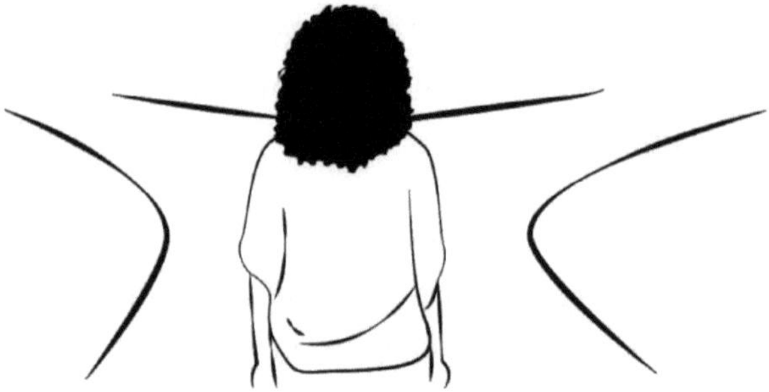

Not much of spark in the start,
Goes unnoticeable however smart.
Encounters mind again and yet again,
Eventually hits ecstasy;
Of pleasure or of pain!
In no time addiction,
Life seems like a prediction.
From day till night,
All the wrong seems right.
A delusion, a phase,
A truth, or a trace.
Seemingly eternal,
A quest or a maze!
Emotional or physical;
In the manner so typical
Hits all the chords
With utmost sheer force
A part then gets lost

Of not him
But of yours
And just as we start to understand,
There comes another one;
That restarts and allures!

THE TWO AND THE ONE

Little faster better,
Those hearts beat.
Wide naked serene,
Those eyes meet.

A lot said, a lot to say,
Years pass by, just like a day;
May to April, April to May,
Mind satisfied & the heart is gay.

Wish there is no end to this game,
Wish it ever remains the same;
Friends, relationships, marriage....
"What's in a name?"

Looking back now
Years that passed
You and I may have moved on
It’s the eternal love that lasts.

LIFE OF A MAGISTRATE

A Dias full of files,
A spectre full of lies;
A situation of instant affray,
Welcome to this ordered disarray!

Eyes, ears, mind, body,
Together come to play;
"SIR, my file is in order,
SIR, my file is in hearing,"
Hey wait, I am Madam by the way!

Brothers disputing ancestral property,
Friends fighting over "trust-laced" cheques;
Somewhere the cruelty has been too much,
Somewhere the recent marriage is in wrecks!

Lawyers, clients, assertions, denials,
Substantive, procedural, extended trials;
The satisfaction of getting there just in time
The soreness that befalls when file lives and life
dies!

Action plan, agendas, meetings all day,
Within a blink of an eye, the next day is in sway;
Still getting on, still working without delay,
To secure the trust of those who believe in this,
who constantly pray!

LIFE'S MEMOIR

When I began you were all cheerful,
Happy to the most and not in the least fearful.
One month and then another,
With vigour you faced the changing weather,
Of getting through life in general,
And exam in particular;
Trodding on a path that makes your own self better!
Managing work and panicking life,
Sometimes you got along, others swayed by strife.
Kept going with all those lows,
Stood your ground amidst those blows.
One after another, life stooped so low,
Despair entangled the bright happier flow.
Lost hope but soon regained it;
'Didn't have any choice' or 'you bargained it',
Some secrets of getting through....
Only you would know!!

It paid off and it was all worth the struggle,
Opening that file, oh your heart quite trembled.
And I still remember that energy and flair,
The strong fever you had suddenly went into the air.
Greetings were on the way and congratulations too. But no one was as happier;
as I was for you ……….

REALISATION

Suddenly I feel air
That is lighter and fair;

Suddenly I feel the voice
That is no longer a noise.
Suddenly I feel emotionally connected
In this social-disconnection;
Peace everywhere, a mental insurrection.

Today when I see, I see the reality;
Breaking off the facade, lingering towards
equality.

Today when I hear, I hear the bird;
Everything sounds clear, every little word.

Today what I touch, it seems so pious;
Like never touched before, like never known
riots!

Today when I smell, I smell the alacrity;
The victory of wholesomeness over brevity.
Suddenly my senses go awry and my pain
vanishes;
For what end else we live,
If not to correct the sufferings and blemishes!

I WALKED

I walked through
I walked from
I walked amidst roses and thorns
Privileges I had no luck with
Accolades here and there I surely adorned

Paths well-known
Paths seldom trod
I walked till I could
I walked by all modes

When I looked straight
I found the motivation
To go high and above
Collect commendations

I walked constant
I walked all tests
I walked in pleasure
I walked in unrest

I walked through struggle
I walked through pain
I walked scorching suns
I walked through torrential rains

When I walked enough
I happily stopped
To finally look back
And admire the travelled track

To lows of life
I was no longer prone
But my heart ached to see
That I walked so much, but I walked alone

FROM SOMEONE TO SOMEONE ELSE

Each dream, oh a story it tells
Of becoming from someone to someone else

From physicist to philosopher
From writer to poet
Sometimes a race to know it all
Sometimes searching the empty void

Sometimes a good person,
Others a great leader.
Sometimes all optimistic,
Others just a believer!

Sometimes selfless, giving it all
Reminiscing memories, taking a fall
Others too selfish, justifying instinct
prioritising only on your self precinct.

A race against time and in no actual time
A race against all but only against thine
Continuous dreams, continuous chase
We think it too much when it was only a phase.

In each part of our lives, a dream dwells!
And each time of our lives, a story it tells;
Of becoming from someone to someone else!

HURT OR HEART

Hey hi wassup
Regular chatting is nice
But let's do a call if you are up!
Oh sure, why not
There is nothing urgent, that I have got
Didn't feel like we talked for the first time
Not just the outside, your inside too felt sublime.
Why does it feel like a complete part of me
My heart isn't aching, it's dancing in glee
Is this real, we are more than just friends
One month, then two, feels like our souls have blend.
Do you feel it, feel the same way?
You make me smile almost everyday.
Yes yes, I do.

I feel everything
That's happening with you.
Six months into it
I was assured it was my best start
For he feels with me
Even when we are miles apart
To ask to move on to the next step
I thought it to be the right time
Suddenly it all went haywire
started off as a broken rhyme
He said, what's happened to me
Why am I going on a nonsensical spree
Did I say anything like that
Did I promise anything to you
Apart from temporarily enjoying this
Did I say to spend the rest of my life too.
Then why this eccentricity
What's this delusional phase
You "repel" me, give me some space
I tried to talk he didn't respond
Picked up my calls but that reciprocity was gone
I tried to calm down, tried to understand
When I failed at where I was wrong
As I started feeling at once alone
No reply, again a text.
No call, same thing the day next
Days and days passed by.
Didn't just feel tired, felt it was all a lie.
Hurts this almost everyday now

But at least now I know
To not fall into this again
I end this today with this vow.

ONE DAY

One day, one asked another,
Excuse me, can I have you bother?

Surprised and shocked as he was,
She tried to make him understand her cause.

But mesmerised at the beauty,
He forgot to do his duty.

She ended her tale at the end of an hour,
But he couldn't fathom a word,
just stunned at the power.

And then comes the cry,
When she asked him something similar to
"WHY"?

Surely it was something related to the
conversation
And now he got to answer,
can't rule it out to negation.

Having nothing to say, he felt guilty,
Maybe I could have listened, could have used
the ability.

But now it's all over,
And he sank in his eyes even lower.
And then.......
One day, one asked another,
Excuse me, can I have you bother!!!!!

ALTHOUGH……BUT

Although going on romantic dinner dates at
fancy restaurants is fulfilling,
But, sitting on that couch closer to you and
eating food cooked together is much more
satisfying.

Although receiving gifts from you every now
and then is fulfilling;
But the affection and caress I feel when with you
is much more satisfying.

Although the Instagram posts, the PDAs, are fulfilling,
But having an understanding with you on a deeper level is much more satisfying.

Although sharing all your happy moments with you is fulfilling,
But the one you seek when you feel low is much more satisfying.

Although being with you in this moment is fulfilling,
But living a lifetime with you is much more satisfying.

SOMETHING, SOMEONE, SOMEWHERE

Stop hurting it anymore,
This heart, so pure!
Spare the endless pain,
Which these eyes endure.

This isn't any game,
To play fair or foul,
Oh, poor creature;
Don't sadden this soul!

Dont seek, don't wait,
Don't fight, don't abate,
Hold on just once more;
Once more, just don't break!

Something, someone, somewhere,
Who will know to take care;
Trust yourself for this,
"Is" and "will be" there.

FIRSTS

As the time is nearing,
The heart with heavy bearing,
Says not a lot,
But feels all reels;
Of these almost four year journey,
Which is way more than just my ‘first’ earning!
A dream fulfilled.
All desires taken care of;
Brought out someone I never knew existed,
A real-life learning!
‘Firsts’ as they say,
Are there to stay.
And this “first “concludes,
My most important fray!!
The head may forget,
Since retaining capacities are rare;
But the phase I lived here,
In my heart;
Is and will always be there.

DREAMS' DILEMMAS

And then sometimes I think,
I could have escaped when it was time.
Or probably even now,
Even now if I could escape.
To somewhere far;
not just far in the worldly terms,
But far on the inside.
Leaving all this consciousness behind
And take another.
One that would be a lot easier,
Or even not easier;
then better.
Better than this one!

But whose?
And where?

Trips to foreign lands!
Wear those expensive brands.

A crazy amount of cash?
Or all the time in my hands.

How would I like that?
I even spoke about it back once;
When across that silent river I sat.
My lips weren't moving much,
But my heart was throbbing at its best.

Those thundering beats making noises of all sorts.
While I was craving to decipher any meaning therefrom!

But alas, there was none.
But alas, there were many.
Are there any choices?
Or is it all a planning!

And I got up from that riverside,
No answers yet but I had my pride.
And I looked above to that tallest tree,
Ok! Retain my consciousness, but make it free!

And while my eyes were making this telepathic resonance;
My reality was paying my dream its condolence.

How much I wanted to not wake up, stay here.
What's the purpose of living in this limited
sphere?

This is when the thought again popped up!
But whose?
And where?

MONSOON

As a child back then, I was always fascinated by rain,
Monsoon, that part of the year, I would always crave.

My little wide eyes kept awaiting those dark clouds,
My heart would always skip a beat at those thundering shouts.

Then be it that heavy instant downpour,
that eclipses everything behind;
or the constant continuous drizzles,
A sight always to long for.

Those falling droplets were as silent as they were loud
The landscape afterwards was as peaceful as it was proud!

Underneath that vast humongous sky,
It seemed all my dreams and realities lie.

As to why it was so,
The answer still eludes me;
But I am grown up now,
But this weather, to be honest;
Still seduce me!

Printed by Libri Plureos GmbH in Hamburg, Germany

9 789363 311411